Minority Soldiers Fighting in the Civil War

JOEL NEWSOME

Cavendish
Square

New York

Published in 2018 by Cavendish Square Publishing, LLC
243 5th Avenue, Suite 136, New York, NY 10016

Website: cavendishsq.com

This publication represents the opinions and views of the author based on his or her personal
experience, knowledge, and research. The information in this book serves as a general guide
only. The author and publisher have used their best efforts in preparing this book and
disclaim liability rising directly or indirectly from the use and application of this book.

CPSIA Compliance Information: Batch #CS17CSQ

All websites were available and accurate when this book was sent to press.

Library of Congress Cataloging-in-Publication Data

Names: Newsome, Joel.
Title: Minority soldiers fighting in the Civil War / Joel Newsome.
Description: New York : Cavendish Square, 2018. | Series: Fighting
for their country: minorities at war | Includes index.
Identifiers: ISBN 9781502626622 (library bound) | ISBN 9781502626561 (ebook)
Subjects: LCSH: United States--History--Civil War, 1861-1865--Juvenile literature. | United
States. Army--African American troops--History--19th century--Juvenile literature. | United
States--History--Civil War, 1861-1865--African Americans--Juvenile literature. | United
States--History--Civil War, 1861-1865--Participation, African American--Juvenile literature.
Classification: LCC E468.N49 2018 | DDC 973.7--dc23

Editorial Director: David McNamara
Editor: Caitlyn Miller
Copy Editor: Alex Tessman
Associate Art Director: Amy Greenan
Designer: Stephanie Flecha
Production Coordinator: Karol Szymczuk
Photo Research: J8 Media

CONTENTS

A Nation Divided

T hroughout history, many societies have depended upon marginalized minority citizens to defend their nations in times of conflict. Yet the American Civil War is unique. Slavery, the conflict that sparked the war, was central to the lives of the largest minority population in the young United States: African Americans. Though there were free black communities in the United States, the vast majority of black Americans were enslaved at the time of the war. As **abolitionist** movements grew and the country expanded westward, the future of the so-called peculiar institution inspired vehement debate. Slaveholders advocated for legal slavery in new territories and harsher penalties for runaway slaves and their supporters, while abolitionists envisioned the end of human bondage in the United States.

Opposite: **John S. Parker, pictured here, was one of thousands of African Americans who rushed to enlist in the armed forces.**

In 1619, the first kidnapped Africans were delivered to the colony of Jamestown, Virginia. African slaves were trafficked to help grow crops, such as tobacco and rice. As the slave trade grew, the institution of slavery spread throughout the early American colonies. More than one hundred and fifty years before the Declaration of Independence was signed, slavery was already a cornerstone of the fledgling American economy. The slave trade was a massive international operation that immediately flourished: historians have estimated that between six and seven million Africans were kidnapped and transported to the United States in the eighteenth century.

After the American Revolution, many Northern cities began to distance themselves from the institution of slavery, and the abolitionist movement started as its first proponents called for an end to legal human bondage. Yet Northerners still enjoyed the fruits of slave labor, getting rich on Southern investments or simply being able to afford cheap goods priced as the result of free labor, though the institution of slavery was not as widespread in the North as it was in the Southern states whose economy depended upon agriculture.

By the late 1700s, the price of tobacco fell, and Southerners felt the squeeze of a dragging economy. In 1792, a recent graduate of Yale University, Eli Whitney, moved from New England to a Georgia plantation to work as a private tutor. Whitney soon discovered that Southern farmers were in desperate need of a way to make cotton a profitable crop. The problem was that the vast majority of cotton grew with sticky seeds that had to be removed from the fluffy boll. Removing the seeds was time consuming and limited the amount of cotton that could be effectively harvested. Whitney invented a machine that removed the seeds from unprocessed cotton in a fraction of the time it took to do so by hand.

Whitney's invention of the cotton gin invigorated the Southern economy and increased the Southern demand for slave labor exponentially. While the cotton gin did the work of separating the seeds from the boll, enslaved people still grew and harvested the crop. The young American economy flourished along with slavery. Cotton was grown in the South but shipped to the North to be processed and woven into clothing and other goods. Between 1790 and 1860, the number of slave states increased from six to fifteen. Congress banned the international slave trade in 1808, but over the next fifty years, the enslaved population almost tripled. While the international slave trade was prohibited, the domestic slave trade was alive and well. By 1860, there were more than four million enslaved people living in the United States. The majority were located in Southern states and accounted for a third of the South's total population.

While slavery expanded in the South with the arrival of Whitney's cotton gin, the question of westward expansion loomed over the land. Bloody conflicts between civilians raged in new territories while the United States government struggled to produce a solution that would appease slaveholders and end the violence among white citizens. Though history remembers the Civil War as the conflict that "freed the slaves," the majority of white Americans who lived through it did not agree that the war was fought over human bondage. Many white people viewed the war as a conflict about states' rights and resented the idea that African Americans should be liberated. As the bloodiest war in American history raged, the question of

The cotton gin led to the expansion of slavery.

whether or not to free and arm African Americans was met with suspicion and derision by many white people in both the Union and the Confederacy.

Though black soldiers had served in the War of 1812 and the Revolutionary War, African Americans were initially barred from service for the first two years of the Civil War. Some African Americans found ways to serve, passing for white men or leading missions of their own design. After finally being allowed to enlist, black soldiers faced harsh treatment and public ridicule. Many were recruited in secret and, once they began their service, they were denied equal pay.

Eventually, more than 179,000 black soldiers served in the Union Army and 19,000 more served in the navy. While African Americans were present behind Confederate lines, they often did manual labor or served as hand servants for specific officers. Native Americans, on the other hand, were recruited by the Confederacy to fight in the area between Kansas and Texas, known as Indian Territory, in an effort to distract Union forces from the more vital theaters of war.

The following chapters explore the lives of minority soldiers, what circumstances were like before the war, where and how minority soldiers served in battle, and how their lives changed once the war ended. These soldiers fought valiantly for their country; ultimately, they succeeded in fighting for freedoms of their own.

Life Before the War

Prior to the Civil War, African Americans suffered the harsh realities of slavery and mass discrimination. Many African Americans resisted slavery through abolitionist efforts and risky attempts at escape. At the same time, the United States government legislated the expansion and preservation of the institution. While African Americans experienced horrific tragedy and brutal consequences for attempting to assert their humanity, they did not give up the hope of freedom.

THE FIGHT FOR FREEDOM

The institution of slavery in the United States was dependent upon the control and subjugation of enslaved people. However, some slaves did revolt against the horrible conditions they were forced to live under. Some used weapons and violence in their fight against injustice, while others attempted to secure their freedom through the legal system.

Opposite: African slaves were often forced to work cotton fields in the South.

Nat Turner

Nat Turner was a black preacher enslaved in Virginia. He believed that he had received divine instruction to mount a rebellion, and he took an eclipse of the sun in 1831 as a sign that the time had come. Turner and six of his followers killed their master and his family, obtained weapons and horses, and gathered seventy-five other slaves to participate in a chaotic insurrection that killed fifty-one white people. Afterwards, Turner hid for about six weeks before being discovered by a local farmer. He was hanged along with fifty-six other slaves accused of participating in the insurrection.

Though the rebellion was ultimately suppressed, it struck fear into the hearts of slaveholders and Southern whites alike.

This illustration created by William Henry Shelton depicts the capture of Nat Turner.

More than two hundred African Americans who did not participate in the rebellion were beaten by local white people angered and frightened by Turner's insurrection. Nat Turner's rebellion was often pointed to as a reason for supporting stricter legislation regarding everything from prohibiting the education of slaves to harsher punishments for aiding runaways. Southern fear did not subside with the passage of time, and legislation would continue to reflect white interest in suppressing slave rebellions.

This interest cropped up again and again as the United States expanded. In 1850, the California gold rush began, and the population of what is now the state of California soared. Its residents applied to enter the Union as a free state, or one that would not allow the practice of slavery. Southerners resisted acknowledging California unless slavery was allowed there. The **Compromise of 1850** attempted to appease pro-slavery interests while still admitting California into the Union. In exchange for designating California as a free state and ending the slave trade (but not slavery itself) in Washington, DC, firmer fugitive slave laws were established. The laws made it easier for slave owners to track down and return runaway slaves to bondage.

The **Fugitive Slave Law of 1850** was a result of the compromise and was one of the harshest pieces of legislature ever passed by the United States Congress. Under the law, US officials and ordinary citizens alike were obligated to assist in seizing suspected fugitive slaves. If they did not comply, citizens could be fined or imprisoned. African Americans and some whites were horrified by the barbaric law and many were drawn to abolitionism as a result.

The Dred Scott Decision

In 1856, the case of *Dred Scott v. Sanford* reached the Supreme Court. Dred Scott had been a slave owned by an army doctor in Missouri. The doctor traveled often and took Scott along when he did, moving between Missouri (a slave state) and free states. Upon the doctor's death, Scott filed for his freedom citing the fact that he had been transported to territory where slavery was illegal. Therefore, he said, he would have to be considered a free man. The Supreme Court's disagreement with Scott was devastating to abolitionists. Not only did the Court proclaim that Scott was not free, it went so far as to state that Congress had no authority to prevent slave owners from taking their slaves into any territory they wished, essentially legalizing slavery throughout the country.

THE HORRORS OF THE ANTEBELLUM SOUTH

The period before the Civil War in Southern states is often referred to as the **antebellum** South. At that time, a household might have one or two slaves to take care of children and cook for the family, or a slave might work alone serving a single master. In some instances, slaves worked on large plantations, though many plantations held less than fifty slave laborers. A variety of regulations ensured that slaves remained dependent on white "owners." For instance, it was illegal for a slave to learn to read and write. Anyone suspected of violating this mandate faced harsh punishments; Southern whites understood that literacy would give slave laborers the **agency** to seek freedom.

Daily life for slaves was excruciating. Slave auctions separated family members from one another and treated this as a routine transaction. Slaves were branded to display that they were property. Some slaves bore several brands, a brutal history of ownership. Men in bondage were purchased specifically for heavy labor while women were selected for their perceived fertility. Women in their child-bearing years were attractive to slave holders because their children also became a slave owner's property. Female slaves were subject to both physical assaults and sexual degradation. One-third of slaves in South Carolina died within a year of their arrival. Two-thirds of enslaved children died before the age of sixteen. Despite abysmal survival rates, by the time the Civil War began, four million people were living in bondage.

The instruments of slavery were torturous. Iron shackles clanged around slaves' wrists and ankles. Some were even muzzled. Punishment was meted out indiscriminately with a variety of weapons, and many slave handlers opted to lash their charges with a whip. After being flogged, an irritant, such as salt, was often rubbed into the offending slave's fresh wounds.

Deprived of their names, education, family, culture, traditions, and a proper home, African Americans in bondage experienced unimaginable violence. For some, daily life was so horrific that they took their chances and gambled on escaping the clutches of slavery.

William Chin, pictured here, was forced into slavery, branded by his captors, and subdued using iron chains, collars, and handcuffs.

ESCAPE VIA THE UNDERGROUND RAILROAD

In America's early years, as slavery was beginning to expand, free African Americans and some religious white people began shepherding slaves out of bondage towards the Northern United States and Canada. In 1786, George Washington himself lamented the loss of a slave who had run away with the aid of "society of Quakers, formed for such purposes." This loose network of safe houses and transport, which was run largely by African Americans, grew over the years. In 1831, it came to be known as the Underground Railroad. Though the Underground Railroad was not a railroad at all, the emerging steam rail system offered coded jargon used to refer to the system's parts. For example, safe stops along the way were referred to as stations or depots, and the people who ran them were considered stationmasters. Conductors were those responsible for transporting fugitives from station to station. While the system stretched across fourteen states and Canada, organizers knew only of the local efforts to aid fugitives and not the overall system. This secrecy kept the system safely running for years despite the capture of some fugitives and stations.

The Underground Railroad offered support for fleeing slaves; however, the journey was incredible risky and failure would likely result in death. Conductors (usually free African Americans) were sometimes dispatched to plantations to lead fugitives to the nearest station, but often slaves had to rely on their own cunning and resourcefulness to reach their first station. Fugitive slaves often began their journeys under the cover of darkness with nothing but the North Star to guide them. Once fugitives reached a station, they often needed new clothing in order to draw less suspicion from the public. A black person in tattered rags was far more likely to be stopped and questioned. White abolitionist groups donated funds to secure inconspicuous clothing, food, and other resources for escaped slaves.

While it is hard to say how many African Americans found their way to freedom via the Underground Railroad, scholars believe that, at the very least, hundreds escaped every year. Some estimates suggest that the South lost over 100,000 slaves between 1810 and 1850. Harriet Tubman was one individual who singlehandedly saved hundreds of enslaved African Americans.

Harriet Tubman

Undoubtedly the most famous conductor of the Underground Railroad, Harriet Tubman was an escapee who had freed herself from bondage. Tubman was born into slavery on Maryland's Eastern Shore. She worked as a field hand and endured horrific beatings until she fled in 1849. She left her husband and family for freedom and proceeded to make at least nineteen trips back to the South to usher other runaways towards the North. As stories of her exploits circulated, bounties were placed on her head, reaching up to $40,000. Nevertheless, Tubman eluded capture and, during all her years aiding fugitives, she never lost a slave and never allowed one to turn back.

Tubman used her knowledge of local areas, her meek appearance, her ever-present pistol, and her faith in God to evade bounty hunters. Once the Civil War began, Union forces appealed to Tubman for assistance in the war effort. She served as a spy, scout, and nurse while the war raged.

Harriet Tubman escaped slavery and spent the next fifteen years helping over three hundred slaves find freedom.

Tubman helped over three hundred slaves attain freedom during her time as a conductor on the Underground Railroad. She also assisted John Brown in planning his raid on Harper's Ferry, nursed soldiers and citizens both black and white, and assisted Union forces in several raids on Southern coastal areas.

Considering the number of enslaved people who remained in bondage, the number of those who escaped seems paltry. However, the knowledge that runaway slaves were being aided by outside organizers frightened and infuriated proslavery citizens. It also gave hope to those who remained imprisoned by the cruel system of slavery.

THE ABOLITIONIST MOVEMENT

While slaves continued to seek freedom through daring escape and **freedmen** labored to create meaningful lives under crushing prejudice, a movement of concerned citizens focused on ending slavery mounted.

Frederick Douglass

Though the Abolitionist movement had been growing in America since the Revolutionary War, abolitionists struggled to sway many white people who had never come face to face with slavery. Men like William Lloyd Garrison gave stirring speeches and published newspapers about the evils of forced servitude, but these efforts lacked the nuance and texture of an authentic experience. Frederick Douglass lent his recollection of slavery's tyranny and his personal struggles to the Abolitionist effort, breathing new life into antislavery pursuits.

Douglass was born around 1818 on Maryland's Eastern Shore and named Frederick Augustus Washington Bailey. His mother was a slave, and all he knew of his father was that he was white. His early years were spent with his grandparents, and he saw his mother only four or five times before her death. He witnessed brutal beatings and was cold and starved for much of the first seven years of his life. At eight years old, he was sent to Baltimore, where he learned to read. He read newspapers voraciously, and it was in Baltimore that Douglass was first exposed to the term abolitionist, though he had no idea that he would become a world-famous spokesperson for the movement.

In his teenage years, Douglass was sent to work for Edward Covey, a man with a reputation as a "slave breaker," who beat Douglass mercilessly. Douglass fought back eventually and after besting Covey in a fight, he was never beaten by Covey again. Douglass attempted to escape slavery twice before he finally succeeded. In 1838, he posed as a sailor with a uniform he had received from a free black woman named Anna Murray and identification papers he had obtained from a free black seaman. Douglass boarded a train and arrived in a safe house in New York. There he sent for Anna and they married, settling in New Bedford, Massachusetts. They adopted the name Douglass (he was still known as Frederick Bailey at the time), and the couple became immersed in the thriving free black community and began attending abolitionist meetings. Eventually, Douglass was asked to share his experiences as a slave. Under the guidance of William Lloyd Garrison, an active abolitionist publisher and speaker, Douglass became a regular lecturer. He traveled across the country offering his experience as a slave as evidence of the institution's degradation and immorality. His viewpoint gave invaluable authenticity to a movement that had largely depended on white orators speaking about an evil in abstract terms.

Seeking a broader audience for his work, Douglass published his autobiography in 1845. *Narrative of the Life of Frederick Douglass, an American Slave* was immensely popular and became a bestseller in the United States. In the book, Douglass details his exposure to slavery's cruelty in his early years, learning to read, and his fight with Edward Covey. Because Douglass elected to name his former masters, the popularity of his work put him in danger. As old masters dismissed his narrative and issued increased bounties for his recapture, Douglass traveled overseas. He traveled around Europe speaking against the evils of slavery for two years. During this time, his supporters in Britain collected funds for the purchase of Douglass's freedom, allowing him to return to the United States in 1847 as a free man.

Upon his return, Douglass began publishing abolitionist newspapers including *The North Star, Frederick Douglass Weekly, Frederick Douglass' Paper, Douglass' Monthly,* and *New National Era.* He was a very early supporter of the women's **suffrage** movement and attended the first women's rights convention in 1848. He frequently spoke about the necessity of suffrage for both women and African Americans.

Frederick Douglass was an abolitionist author and orator who pressured Abraham Lincoln to move toward emancipation and dedicated his life to civil rights struggles.

As a result of Douglass's written works and skilled oratory, he was a very famous abolitionist voice by the beginning of the Civil War. Though the dissolution of the union made many Northern whites anxious about the future of the country, Douglass encouraged secession. As the war dragged on, Douglass ceaselessly advocated for abolition and for black service in the Union army.

Harriet Beecher Stowe

While Frederick Douglass converted many hearts and minds to the abolitionist resistance by offering his firsthand account of slavery's degradation, other abolitionists penned works that opened the eyes of the ignorant through fictional storytelling. The most notable author to employ fiction in the service of exposing slavery's horrors was Harriet Beecher Stowe.

The death of Stowe's beloved child in 1849 along with the Fugitive Slave Act in 1850 inspired her to write an anti-slavery novel. She searched newspapers and slave narratives for firsthand descriptions of slavery and began to compile what would become her most famous work. Her first installment of **Uncle Tom's Cabin** was published on June 5th, 1851, in the abolitionist newspaper *The National Era*. A year later it was published as a two-volume book and sold three hundred thousand copies in its first year; it has been translated into over sixty languages. Though it reads as sentimental—and at times racist—by today's standards, the novel successfully conveyed the necessity of abolition to many readers.

John Brown

The vast majority of abolitionists favored a nonviolent approach to ending slavery, so John Brown's violent opposition to the institution shocked the country and pushed the United States to reckon with slavery's evils.

Born to an extremely religious family in 1800, John Brown spent his childhood listening to his father's abolitionist views. Though he was a transient man who would hold a variety of jobs and declare bankruptcy at the age of forty, John Brown spent his life and what little money he had fighting slavery. He was an active supporter of the Underground Railroad, gave land to runaway slaves, and established the League of Gileadites, an organization that helped escaped slaves make their way to Canada.

In 1855, he moved with his sons to the Kansas Territory, where he was an active participant in giving Kansas its new nickname: Bleeding Kansas. After a proslavery raid on Lawrence, Kansas, Brown responded with his own coldblooded violence. With the assistance of his sons, Brown dragged five unarmed men who were believed to be slavery supporters from their home and slaughtered them on May 24th, 1856. Soon afterward, Brown traveled to Missouri and freed eleven slaves, killing their master. For two years, Brown traveled New England gathering donations to support his efforts. He planned to bring his war against slavery to the South, initiated with a raid of Harper's Ferry, Virginia. In 1859, Brown rented a farmhouse four miles north of Harper's Ferry and commenced training a small army that consisted of twenty-one men, both white and black. He planned to capture the arsenal at Harper's Ferry and to then arm local slaves who would join their efforts and free more slaves as they advanced south along the Appalachian Mountains. Brown believed his plan would strike fear into the hearts of Southern slave owners and bring about the end of human bondage in the United States.

Though Brown's plan was ambitious, it did not succeed. The attempted raid on the federal arsenal at Harper's Ferry took place on October 16th, 1859. Local militia and the United States Marines led by Robert E. Lee quickly suppressed the uprising, killing or capturing most of Brown's men, including two of his sons. Brown was swiftly tried and convicted of murder, inciting slave insurrection, and treason against the state of Virginia. Though he was seriously wounded, John Brown spoke eloquently during the trial. At his sentencing, he said, "If it is deemed necessary that I should forfeit my life for the furtherance of the ends of justice, and mingle my blood further with the blood of my children and with the blood of millions in this slave country whose rights are disregarded by wicked, cruel, and unjust enactments—I submit; so let it be done!"

John Brown was hanged on December 2nd, 1859. He offered these prophetic words in a note handed to his jailer shortly before his death, "I John Brown am now quite certain that the crimes of this guilty, land: will never be purged away; but with Blood. I had as I now think: vainly flattered myself that without very much bloodshed; it might be done."

Crispus Attucks

While neither army was initially interested in enlisting black men in the Civil War, African Americans had fought courageously in both the American Revolution and the War of 1812. In fact, the very first man to die in the Revolutionary War happened to be a young man of color by the name of Crispus Attucks. Attucks was a fugitive slave who ran from Framingham, Massachusetts, to nearby Boston. Historians believe Attucks's father was black, his mother Native American. In Boston, Attucks made his living as a seaman and firmly opposed British Parliament's trade restrictions.

On March 5th, 1770, Attucks and a gathering mob taunted British soldiers, tensions rose, and Crispus Attucks hit a soldier. This prompted the Brits to fire on the mob, killing Attucks. Samuel Adams and other noted Boston residents declared him the first martyr killed by the oppressive British. Attucks's coffin was carried along with three others to Faneuil Hall where Bostonians flocked to pay their respects to those killed in what became known as the Boston Massacre. Crispus Attucks became a symbol of black patriotism. His sacrifice inspired the African Americans in Cincinnati who organized to resist the Fugitive Slave Law; they referred to themselves as Attucks Guards.

A year later, Southern states would secede from the Union, initiating the bloody conflict Brown had predicted.

THE LONG MARCH TOWARD WAR

Though slavery had been present in the United States prior to its inception, the proposed expansion of slavery to new territories, coupled with religious opposition to the cruel institution, divided the United States. Thriving free black communities and abolitionist leaders worked to bring about the end of slavery while the United States government tried to strike a compromise with slaveholders in the interest of preserving the union. In the end, no compromise could be reached. By 1861, the country had plunged into the bloodiest conflict it had ever seen.

The War Itself

The Civil War stretched from the Confederate assault on Fort Sumter in April of 1861 to Robert E. Lee's surrender to Ulysses S. Grant at Appomattox Courthouse on May 9th, 1865. In a little over four years, the country lost an astounding 625,000 men. Upwards of 10,500 engagements occurred during the war, including at least 50 major battles. More American soldiers died in the Civil War than in World War I, World War II, the Korean War, and the Vietnam War combined. Two percent of the US population perished in a war that pitted brother against brother.

A TENSE ELECTION

With the issue of slavery's expansion into western territories splitting public opinion, the presidential election of 1860 saw the campaigns of four different candidates. The Democratic Party split into Northern and Southern factions, nominating

Opposite: This painting by Francis Bicknell Carpenter depicts the first reading of the Emancipation Proclamation before Abraham Lincoln's cabinet.

Stephen Douglas and John C. Breckenridge, respectively. The Constitutional Union Party, a reconvening of the **defunct** Whig Party, nominated John Bell of Tennessee. As a result of the split Democratic Party, Abraham Lincoln, the Republican nominee, was guaranteed victory. While Lincoln tried to convince Southern whites that he had no interest in ending slavery in those states where it was already practiced, Southerners vehemently opposed a Lincoln presidency. Those with an interest in protecting slavery believed Lincoln would abolish the peculiar institution, and talk of revolution was widespread in the weeks leading up to the election.

On November 6th, 1860, Southerners were outraged by Lincoln's official election to the presidency of the United States. Some black leaders who had supported Lincoln's candidacy were inspired by the win. Before the official result, Frederick Douglass had written that Lincoln's presidency "must and will be hailed as an anti-slavery triumph." After Lincoln secured the victory, Douglass went so far as to call for the secession of the Southern slave-holding states: "I am for dissolution of the Union—decidedly for a dissolution of the Union!" Southern landowners were in agreement, and on December 20th, 1861, South Carolina was the first of the southern states to secede.

THE PROCESSION OF SECESSION

By February of the next year, six other states had joined South Carolina. Alabama, Florida, Louisiana, Georgia, Texas, and Mississippi, along with South Carolina, formed the Confederate States of America and chose Montgomery, Alabama, as their capital. Jefferson Davis was selected as their president, and the United States watched to see if a military conflict would develop. Meanwhile, Lincoln focused on reassuring Southerners. In his inaugural address on March 4th, 1861, Lincoln said, "I have no purpose, directly or indirectly, to interfere with the institution of slavery in the States where it exists. I believe I have no lawful right to do so and I have no inclination to do so." He went on to firmly denounce the actions of the newly formed Confederacy saying, "Plainly, the central idea of secession is the essence of anarchy."

Despite Lincoln's appeals to white Southerners to remain with the Union, the damage had been done. A little over a month later, Confederate forces demanded that federal command of Fort Sumter, in the harbor of Charleston, South Carolina, be surrendered. US Army Major Robert Anderson refused, and Confederates open fired on the fort in a hostile act of war. Virginia, North Carolina, Tennessee, and Arkansas joined the Confederate States of America in the wake of the attack. The Confederate States of America moved their capital to Richmond, Virginia, and prepared for the oncoming violence. April 12th, 1861, marked the undisputed end of a perfect union and the beginning of the Civil War.

SEVENTY-FIVE THOUSAND MEN FOR NINETY DAYS OF SERVICE

Once it became clear that the Confederacy would not back down and rejoin the Union, Lincoln put out a call for soldiers. He wanted seventy-five thousand men for ninety days of service, believing like many other Northerners that the war could be fought and won in a matter of weeks. Free African Americans answered Lincoln's call, but they were rejected along with

Native Americans. The Confederacy, on the other hand, would eventually actively recruit Native Americans while resisting arming African Americans until the very end of the war. In 1861, the Civil War was still considered a white man's war and, as the new recruits trained, Lincoln and his generals devised a strategy for what they hoped would be swift defeat.

Northerners began to demand a Union strike in reprisal for the assault on Fort Sumter, so Union forces planned an attack on Richmond, Virginia. The newly formed Confederate Congress was slated to meet in their capital, and Lincoln ordered Brigadier General Irvin McDowell to launch an attack that would devastate the enemy quickly and make Richmond available for the taking. Gathered with thirty-five thousand troops in Washington, DC, McDowell was hesitant, citing lack of preparation as a reason to postpone the onslaught. Lincoln could not be swayed; he reasoned that Confederate soldiers were also relatively new to military training. Lincoln ordered McDowell to begin the march towards Manassas Junction, Virginia, and a small river known as Bull Run. Manassas Junction was located just 25 miles (40.2 kilometers) outside of Washington, DC, and several civilians decided to enjoy the beautiful July day by accompanying their soldiers to battle and watching them fight to victory while they lunched from picnic baskets.

McDowell knew that there would be at least twenty thousand Confederate troops camped near Bull Run that he would have to overwhelm in order to continue toward Richmond. What he didn't know was that Confederate forces had caught wind of the movement of Union forces and were already sending for reinforcements before the Union had even arrived at Bull Run. Eleven thousand more troops made their way toward the river in anticipation of the first major land battle of the civil war.

THE FIRST BATTLE OF BULL RUN

Union forces clashed with Confederate soldiers at Bull Run for the first time on July 21st, 1861. For the first two hours of the conflict, the Northerners pushed Confederates back gradually, and initially the battle looked to be quickly turning into a Union victory. However, Confederate reinforcements soon arrived and rallied the Southern troops. They attacked fervently, crying out as they advanced on the Union soldiers. This battle cry would become known as the rebel yell. Eventually, the Confederates managed to break the Union line and sent the Northern soldiers fleeing across the river, colliding with their picnicking supporters who were busy making their own escape.

Though Union forces retreated, Confederate troops were too disorganized to pursue the fleeing soldiers and the Northerners were able to reach the safety of Washington, DC. There were around three thousand Union casualties at the First Battle of Bull Run; the Confederates suffered fewer than two thousand. The violence left Northerners who had expected a quick end to the war devastated, and it emboldened Confederates who began to believe they could bring about a swift victory. Confederate leaders bickered about who was at fault for the failure to successfully pursue the enemy while Lincoln relieved McDowell of command and selected George B. McClellan as his replacement.

THE QUESTION OF BLACK FREEDOM

Though African Americans had been refused the right to serve in the Union army, the question of what to do with runaway slaves was posed almost immediately after the Civil War had begun. A month after the beginning of the war, slaves who had been working on construction of Confederate forts in Virginia escaped and fled to the Union's Fort Monroe. Their owner arrived the next day demanding his slaves be returned under the 1850 Fugitive Slave Act. Union Major General Benjamin Butler informed him that because Virginia was no longer loyal to the Union, the law was invalid. Butler did not return the escaped slaves, nor did he free them. Instead, Butler declared the fugitives **contraband**, or enemy property, and allowed them to stay at Fort Monroe and work for the Union. Runaways began to flock to Fort Monroe and outbreaks of tuberculosis and dysentery plagued the crowded encampments. Nevertheless, escapees continued to arrive and began to educate themselves as they enjoyed their first taste of freedom.

On August 6th, 1861, Congress passed the **First Confiscation Act**, clarifying the status of fugitive slaves. The act stated that Federal forces could seize any property used by the Confederacy in the war effort. Thus, only those slaves who were found to be working in service of the military effort would be freed. Union General John C. Fremont went beyond the limits of the legislation and immediately freed all the slaves belonging to Confederates in Missouri. Lincoln voided the decree and informed Fremont that only slaves who were being actively used to aid the Confederates were to be freed.

In May of 1862, General David Hunter proclaimed the end of slavery in Florida, Georgia, and South Carolina. Though Lincoln revoked the order, thousands of slaves along the coast escaped to Union camps while many plantation owners fled inland.

Lincoln feared that freeing the slaves would lead Missouri or Kentucky to join the Confederacy, so he proceeded with extreme caution. Black leaders grew frustrated with Lincoln and voiced their concerns that the president might never bring an end to slavery; Lincoln remained resolute. He held fast to the belief that the best way to end slavery in the United States was through compensated emancipation followed by the colonization of former slaves outside of the United States. He tried to convince states bordering the Confederacy, who were vulnerable to secession, to support his plan for gradual emancipation as a means of ensuring that they did not secede. Lincoln's proposal was incredibly unpopular among whites and blacks alike. White slave holders wanted to continue profiting from human bondage while black Americans had no interest in being shipped to a foreign land. Though Lincoln would waver for years to come, it was becoming clear that the war could not end without slavery ending with it.

In August of 1862, Lincoln summoned black leaders to Washington in order to persuade them that colonization outside the United States following emancipation was the best solution to the problem of American racism. After denouncing the evils of slavery, Lincoln went on to say:

Your race suffer very greatly, many of them, by living among us, while ours suffer from your presence. There is an unwillingness on the part of our people, harsh as it may be, for your free colored people to remain among us ... I do not wish to discuss this, but to propose it as a fact with which we have to deal. I cannot alter it if I would.

Black leaders were offended by Lincoln's solution and responded accordingly. Frederick Douglass explained that supporting colonization would allow whites "to commit all kinds of violence" against African Americans.

Lincoln held fast to his support for colonization, and in 1863, the government attempted to resettle 453 black Americans on an island near Haiti. The results were disastrous as disease and starvation plagued the settlers. The government experiment ended in 1864 when 368 survivors were returned to the United States.

SHILOH

In early April of 1862, the western theater of war would see its first major battle. Major General Ulysses S. Grant and his Army of the Tennessee made camp at Pittsburg Landing. Grant's amateur troops spent their time training while they awaited the arrival of Major General Don Carlos Buell's Army of Ohio. The plan was to mount an offensive along the Tennessee River once the reinforcements arrived. However, General Albert Sydney Johnston of the Confederacy knew of Grant's location and strategy. He knew he would need to attack Grant quickly, before more Union men arrived. Though the initial assault was planned on April 4th, it was delayed until April 6th. Despite the postponement, the Union forces were caught completely off guard by the Confederate assault on the morning of the charge.

By the afternoon, a few resolute Union troops were able to hold position at a recessed road known as "Hornet's Nest," but the Confederate onslaught continued and they surrounded the Northern soldiers. Buell's men finally began to arrive, and the Union forces rallied. As he was riding forward to lead a Confederate attack, Johnston was struck in the leg. The bullet hit an artery and he quickly bled out, leaving General Pierre G. T. Beauregard in control. When night fell, Beauregard ended the advance.

With an advantage in troop numbers as a result of Buell's arrival, Grant's attack the following morning was no match for the Confederates. The exhausted rebels fought as they retreated, resulting in major Union casualties. In the end, the Union was able to push them back to Corinth, Mississippi, and out of Tennessee. A total of 23,750 casualties were suffered—a little over 13,000 of those were Union. Though they had seen more losses than the Confederates, the battle highlighted a major advantage for the Union: they had more manpower. With more men able and willing to serve as a result of higher populations, the Union was almost assured victory in the war if they were willing to strike decisively and sacrifice some of those troops. The Battle of Shiloh proved that Grant was willing to do just that.

ANTIETAM

On September 17th, 1862, the armies of Robert E. Lee and George McClellan struggled against each other in what would become the single bloodiest day in American history and the first major battle fought in the North during the civil war. The opposing armies fought along Antietam Creek in Sharpsburg, Maryland. On the way to Antietam, one of

George McClellan's men found a copy of Lee's battle plans. This discovery emboldened the normally cautious McClellan. He led his troops in an attack on Lee's left flank, attempting to overwhelm the Confederates, but the Union was unsuccessful. The first few hours of fighting showed neither side had the upper hand. The battle took place largely in a cornfield, and by midday it was strewn with the bodies of dead soldiers. Union troops attacked the center of the Confederate line, resulting in devastating losses, but Confederate reinforcements eventually held off the advance. The next day, Lee withdrew his troops across the Potomac River. The Confederates had suffered around 10,300 casualties to the Union's 12,400. Though the Confederates had retreated, the battle was largely classified as a bloody draw.

Meanwhile, Lincoln was coming closer and closer to realizing that the Union could not be preserved without ending slavery, at least in the Southern states. While he had proposed the **Emancipation Proclamation** to his Cabinet in July, he was counseled to wait to issue it until after a Union victory. Despite the comparable damage both sides endured, the battle was enough of a victory for Lincoln to issue the preliminary Emancipation Proclamation on September 22nd, 1862. The proclamation stated that if the Confederacy did not surrender by January 1st, 1863, then all slaves in the south would be freed.

FOREVER FREE

While the preliminary Emancipation Proclamation gave African Americans hope that soon slavery would be dealt a crushing blow, the rest of the American public resented the fact that the war seemed to be centering on black freedom.

White Southerners engaged in fervent rebellion mocked the proclamation. Many white Northerners refused to admit that the conflict had anything to do with the liberty of slaves; they thought emancipation was not relevant to the issue of states' rights.

Prior to the announcement of impending emancipation, anti-black tensions threatened northern civilians. Irish dockworkers in Cincinnati brought violence into black neighborhoods after they were replaced by black men during a strike of the city's riverfront wharf hands. Irish immigrants also burned a tobacco factory in Brooklyn, New York, where black women and children were employed.

Despite disapproval from the public and political pressure, Lincoln issued the Emancipation Proclamation on January 1st, 1863. Though many thousands of slaves had already freed themselves, the proclamation made it clear that the war could no longer separate the causes of cementing the Union and abolishing slavery's stranglehold on the United States. It further emboldened enslaved people in the Confederacy to seek freedom and was celebrated by abolitionists and blacks all over the country, especially in places like Boston and Philadelphia.

Though the Emancipation Proclamation freed the slaves in Confederate states, it did not end racist attitudes. Freeing the slaves was an important step in formally allowing black people to serve in the Union army, although some had been serving since the war first began. In the coming years, black soldiers would prove their mettle against a tide of racism and disenfranchisement from both the public and the United States military.

BLACK SERVICE

After the Emancipation Proclamation took effect, the question of whether or not to arm black soldiers was pushed to the forefront. Despite the fact that the Militia Act of 1862 had been passed almost six months prior, many whites, both Northern and Southern, opposed the idea of arms in the hands of newly freed African Americans. Yet military leaders could not deny the tactical advantages of a new pool of recruits. African Americans who had been advocating for the ability to fight would finally be officially recognized as soldiers.

In May of 1862, Union General David Hunter, Commander of the Department of the South, began recruitment of former slaves along the South Carolina coast, and when potential recruits refused the invitation to serve, Hunter used his troops to forcibly conscript them, effectively transitioning fugitives to a new form of bondage. Hunter raised a regiment of five hundred men known as the First South Carolina Volunteers. The new soldiers were outfitted in bright red pants, blue coats, and large hats. Hunter set about training the men while he awaited authorization. When none came, Hunter dissolved most of the companies and the former slaves were sent away without pay or homes to return to.

In July, Congress enacted the Militia Act of 1862, authorizing the enlistment of African Americans. Two regiments were raised in Louisiana the following fall. The Native Guards and General Benjamin Butler's Corps d'Afrique were inducted into the United States Army while General Rufus Saxton gained permission to revive Hunter's dispersed companies. Thomas Wentworth Higginson, a white abolitionist who had helped

This illustration was used on Union recruitment posters in the Philadelphia area. The image's slogan urged black men to enlist with the slogan "Come and Join Us Brothers."

fund John Brown's raid on Harper's Ferry, was placed in command and the regiment was inducted into the US Army on Emancipation Day.

Hazards of Military Service

Recruitment was difficult in the North as black people endured violence due to white resentment. Support for black participation in the war effort was limited to undesirable tasks such as building fortifications, carrying supplies, and burying the dead. Some white people slowly began to lobby for African American involvement only as a means of saving the lives of white soldiers who might perish in battle. African Americans attempting to enlist often did so in secret, meeting at local churches under the cover of darkness for the chance to serve their country.

Black soldiers also had to be especially wary of capture by Confederate forces because they were subject to much harsher reprisals. Many black soldiers who found themselves captives of the Confederate forces were swiftly murdered as opposed to being taken as prisoners of war. Others were sold into slavery after being captured. One of the worst massacres of black troops occurred at Fort Pillow on April 12th, 1864. After Union troops had surrendered, the Confederates murdered three hundred black troops and their commander, William F. Bradford.

Protest

African Americans served in segregated regiments that were commanded by white officers. Many white officers were reluctant to take positions that required them to train and command black troops, as they thought it would sully their military careers. Many others believed that black men were incapable of being trained for combat and would flee at the first sight of battle. Black recruits were woefully ill-equipped when compared with their white counterparts and were paid less than white soldiers, despite being promised equal wages.

The United States War Department authorized lower wages for black soldiers under the assumption that they would be used for fatigue work exclusively and not combat. Black soldiers earned $10 per month compared to white soldiers who earned $13 per month. On top of that, black soldiers were charged an extra $3 per month for clothing, reducing their pay to only $7 per month. Black soldiers and some white commanders protested the inequality. The 54th Regiment of Massachusetts refused to accept any wages until they were

The Pillow Hill Massacre claimed the lives of more than three hundred African American soldiers.

paid an equal amount, putting an enormous strain on their families and morale. Sergeant William Walker of South Carolina advocated for his soldiers to also refuse pay; he was charged and convicted of mutiny and executed by firing squad.

Many soldiers also engaged in letter writing campaigns protesting the unfair wages. After two years of benefitting from black soldiers' service, the government compromised and equalized pay retroactively—but only back to January 1st, 1864. Furthermore, the compromise was only supposed to secure more equal pay for men who had never been slaves. Some commanders found a way around this stipulation, encouraging soldiers to take the Quaker Oath, asserting per God's law that they "owed no man unrequited labor on or before the 19th of April 1861." Even with the compromise, the War Department stalled in its release of the funds. Although some African American soldiers were more adequately compensated, others would spend the postwar years in legal battles with the United States trying to secure wages from the very government that had benefitted from their service.

Naval Service

Though African Americans had to wait for the Union army to allow them to serve, the United States Navy never banned their service. The experience of African Americans in the navy was markedly different than those in the army. Probably the biggest difference was that the navy was integrated. While the army had exclusively black regiments led by white officers, black sailors in the navy served alongside white and international sailors. This was partly due to limited space onboard warships. Sailors were able to enlist at any major Atlantic port. Many of these recruits had years of seafaring experience as a result of working as mariners, dockhands, and fishermen. At the height of the war, African Americans made up 23 percent of all sailors serving in the navy.

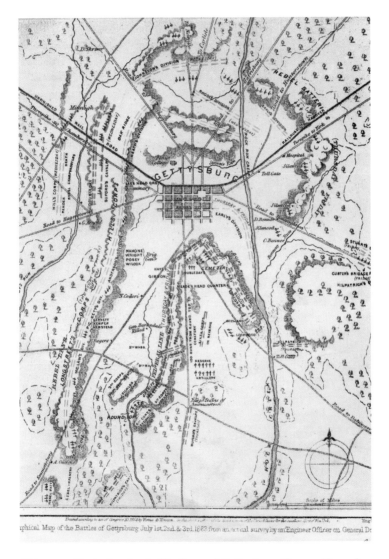

This map illustrates the battle lines at Gettysburg. The position of troops was crucial to this bloody Union victory.

GETTYSBURG

In June of 1863, General Robert E. Lee marched his army of sixty thousand troops into Northern territory with the aim of destroying as many military posts as he could in Maryland and Pennsylvania while Union armies were preoccupied defending Washington, DC. Lee hoped to demoralize Union supporters with a decisive victory on Northern soil. On the march, Lee was notified of a skirmish between Confederate and Union soldiers at Gettysburg, Pennsylvania. Overestimating the number of Union troops present at Gettysburg, Lee ordered all his manpower to march south towards Gettysburg. In the meantime, three thousand Union troops took position along McPherson Ridge and attempted to hold their position while awaiting reinforcements from Washington, DC. The outnumbered Union soldiers were forced to withdraw to Cemetery Ridge, a group of hills to the southeast that form a hook shape. Cemetery Ridge provided a defensive advantage that the Union desperately needed. General Lee saw the challenge that the Union position posed to the Confederate offensive, but because his soldiers still vastly outnumbered Union forces, he pressed on. The battle raged on for days. The position of Union troops combined with the arrival of reinforcements posed an insurmountable challenge to the Confederates: Lee and his men were forced to retreat to Virginia.

An estimated total of 51,100 casualties resulted from the violence at Gettysburg. Though the Confederates had around 5,000 more casualties than the Union, both sides suffered extensive losses. Nevertheless, Gettysburg was a clear Union victory. Four months later, President Lincoln would dedicate the Gettysburg's Soldiers National Cemetery and deliver the famous Gettysburg Address, a short speech honoring the dead and redefining the war's purpose.

VICKSBURG

In the spring of 1862, Union forces set their sights on capturing the **fortified** city of Vicksburg, a strategic location

Vicksburg was a fortified Confederate city along the Mississippi River. Its capture was a striking blow to the rebel South.

on the Mississippi River. Though Grant had attempted to take Vicksburg in the winter of 1861, a renewed effort began in April of the following year. The city sat overlooking the east bank of the Mississippi, and Union officials believed it held the key to occupying the mighty river. The Mississippi lay in front of Grant's army with the delta behind them and the city up on a hill, which proved a challenging position for the Union troops.

Grant attempted a variety of offensive tactics but none worked. Finally, he sent troops down the Mississippi in the middle of the night, and they were able to make it past Vicksburg's artillery. Grant marched the rest of his forces down the west bank of the river, crossed back into Mississippi, defeated Confederate troops in Jackson, and approached Vicksburg from the south, the city's most vulnerable front. Grant's maneuvering allowed him to push Confederate troops into Vicksburg and seal the city off. Once Vicksburg was isolated, the Confederates and civilians within the fortified city were trapped. Grant and his army began a merciless bombardment of the city and residents were forced to retreat to caves to avoid being killed. Over five hundred caves were dug, and Union soldiers mocked the desperate townspeople, dubbing Vicksburg "Prairie Dog Village." The Confederate army made attempts to rescue their trapped compatriots but to no avail. Grant's army of seventy thousand men vastly outnumbered the twenty-nine thousand Confederates inside the city.

As the siege continued, the situation within the perimeter of Vicksburg turned desperate as food supplies waned and people began to starve. Those within the walls ate horses and rats to survive. Ultimately, the siege lasted six weeks, and the Confederates surrendered Vicksburg on July 4th, 1863, a day after the Union victory at Gettysburg. The victory was essential to the Union, effectively splitting the Confederacy and ensuring Union control of the Mississippi River. Upon hearing of the victory, Lincoln was overjoyed. "The father of the waters rolls unvexed to the sea," he proclaimed.

TOTAL WAR

In 1864, Grant took control of all Union troops and, along with Lincoln, devised a strategy to bring about the end of the war as quickly as possible. It was decided that the best way to end conflict would be to declare **total war** on the South. Grant ordered General William Tecumseh Sherman to lead a force through the deep South. Sherman did so with the explicit purpose of creating devastation. So began Sherman's famous **March to the Sea**. He captured Atlanta, the industrial hub of the Confederacy, on September 2nd, 1864. He then led sixty-seven thousand soldiers through Georgia, raiding agriculture and livestock and burning plantations as he went. They marched 285 miles (458.6 km) from Atlanta to Savannah, leaving destruction in their wake. While his soldiers destroyed property and land, neither rape nor unprovoked killings were condoned by Sherman.

Sherman's approach of total war not only destroyed Southern morale, it crippled the Confederate ability to continue the war. Atlanta's capture had already dealt a major blow to Confederate manufacturing and transport. Sherman's march sealed the South's fate by making the very land uninhabitable and striking fear into the hearts of southern civilians and military officials alike. Sherman and his troops reached Savannah on December 21st, 1864. In early 1865, they resumed their march, this time through South Carolina, burning and pillaging as they went toward Charleston. In a matter of months, the Civil War would be over.

THE WAR WINDS DOWN

As General William Tecumseh Sherman devastated Georgia and South Carolina with his March to the Sea, the South lay in shambles. It became impossible for Confederate officials to deny that the end of the war was nearing and that they would not be the victors. Members of the Southern rebellion attempted to negotiate peace terms but were unsuccessful; eventually General Robert E. Lee was forced to surrender to Union forces.

The Hampton Roads Conference

On February 3rd, 1865, President Lincoln met with Confederate representatives in the hopes of negotiating peace terms. They met aboard the steamboat *River Queen* near Hampton, Virginia. The Confederate delegation had hoped that Lincoln might consider ending the war without ending slavery, but Lincoln made it clear that securing peace would require the Confederates to recognize and obey the laws of the Union. Though Lincoln had agreed to the meeting, he was not inclined to make much compromise: the Confederacy was close to collapsing.

Surrender at Appomattox

In April of 1865, Robert E. Lee was on the run from Union forces. The Northerners had been pursuing his retreat for miles, and they had managed to surround the Confederate soldiers. With no escape, Lee had no choice but to send word to Ulysses S. Grant that he was prepared to surrender.

The generals met in the home of a man named Wilmer McLean. McLean had lived near Manassas, Virginia, and had moved his family because he was worried about violence in the area. He had witnessed the first major bloodshed of the Civil War, the First Battle of Bull Run, at his doorstep. Four years later the war was ending in McLean's parlor.

With Lee's surrender, the Civil War was officially over, though there were several skirmishes afterwards. The North rejoiced while the South mourned. Black soldiers and newly freed slaves marched through the streets, joyous at the prospect of an unshackled future.

Anderson Ruffin Abbott

While Americans risked disease, wounds, and death during the Civil War, international soldiers also played a part in the Union Army. Among these foreign fighters was Anderson Ruffin Abbott, Canada's first black physician.

Anderson Ruffin Abbott was born free in Toronto, Ontario, because of his parents' decision to first escape slavery in Alabama and then racism in New York. His father became wealthy after buying land in Toronto, giving Anderson access to the best education. He attended private and public schools, including Oberlin College in the United States. In 1860, he graduated from the Toronto School of Medicine and received his license to practice a year later, making him the first Canadian-born black doctor.

In February of 1863, Abbott applied for an assistant surgeon position in the Union Army. He was rejected but reapplied as a cadet in the United States Colored Troops and began his military career as a civilian surgeon. From 1863 until 1865, he served in a variety of American hospitals, including Freedmen's Hospital, which would become part of Howard University, a historically black college. Later, he was assigned to serve at a hospital in Arlington, Virginia.

Several doctors were present on the night of Lincoln's assassination, and Anderson Ruffin Abbott was one of them. In a gesture of appreciation for attempting to save her late husband's

Anderson Ruffin Abbott, whose parents moved north as a result of racial persecution in the United States, was Canada's first African American physician.

life, Mary Todd Lincoln presented Abbott with a shawl that Lincoln had worn at his first inauguration.

Abbott resigned from his job in Arlington ten years later, though he would return to the United States. He spent the rest of his life fighting against racial segregation and continuing his medical practice. In 1894, he was named the surgeon-in-chief of the first black-owned hospital in the United States. He remained there for just a year before moving back to Toronto, where he died in 1913.

THREE

The 54th Regiment of Massachusetts

I n January of 1863, Secretary of War Edwin Stanton granted John A. Andrew, Governor of Massachusetts, permission to put together a black regiment. Andrew asked several prominent black leaders to lead recruitment efforts as there were very few black men living in Massachusetts. The resulting coalition, known as the Black Committee, included leaders such as Frederick Douglass, Martin Delany, Charles Remond, and Henry Highland Garnet. Together these leaders helped assemble the 54th Regiment of Massachusetts, one of the first government-authorized black units to fight in the Civil War.

The Black Committee recruited men from northern states, including Massachusetts, New York, Indiana, and Ohio. By mid-February nearly a thousand men had enlisted. The recruits came from a variety of professions. Farmers, blacksmiths, butchers, seamen, and others signed on to support the Union on the battlefield. Many of the recruits were literate and, while most

Opposite: This dynamic painting entitled *The Old Flag Never Touched the Ground* features the 54th Regiment storming Fort Wagner.

Located in Boston Common across from the Massachusetts State House, this memorial relief sculpture depicts the march of the 54th Regiment through Boston.

originated from northern states, some hailed from Canada, some from slave states, and some even from the Caribbean. Members of the Black Committee risked their lives and families by denouncing slavery and fighting for black freedom. Frederick Douglass's own sons Charles and Lewis Douglass as well as Martin Delany's son Toussaint volunteered.

Governor Andrew placed Robert Gould Shaw in command of the 54th Massachusetts Regiment. Shaw was the son of two abolitionists and had dropped out of Harvard University to join the Union. A twenty-five-year-old veteran, Shaw had been previously wounded in the Battle of Antietam and was well respected among soldiers.

On May 28th, 1863, almost five months after the Emancipation Proclamation took effect, the 54th Regiment marched through Boston on their way to war. A crowd of thousands lined the streets watching the all-black regiment board a ship that would carry them to war.

The 54th arrived in South Carolina on June 3rd, 1863, and discovered that the US government, while allowing them to fight and possibly die for their country, would not provide equal payment to black soldiers. The soldiers protested the inequality by refusing payment for their services until the wage gap was rectified. Many, including Colonel Robert Gould Shaw, also wrote letters asking for a $3 per month increase.

In addition to unfair wages, the newly trained 54th Regiment was frustrated about being assigned to join Union forces in a raid of Darien, Georgia. Colonel Shaw was deeply disappointed with his fresh recruits' initial experience of the war. He wrote to General George Strong lamenting that his troops had not had the opportunity to fight in battle. Shaw requested that the 54th lead the next Union advance. The newly enlisted men would see battle a month later.

AN ATTEMPT ON FORT SUMTER

The first major test for black Civil War soldiers would involve Fort Sumter. Confederate forces had conducted a massive thirty-four-hour bombardment of the federal stronghold in April of 1861, effectively occupying the fort and beginning the bloody war that black soldiers had only recently been allowed to participate in. Fort Sumter's occupation had long irked the Union Army, and its recapture was seen as a key to victory. One of the major obstacles to taking the fort was a reinforced battery called Fort Wagner. Though Wagner looked like little more than large sand hills, it was actually a protected earthwork installation on Morris Island that obstructed the entrance to the Charleston harbor. Wagner was constructed with sand held in place by soil, sand bags, and palmetto logs. The south wall of Wagner was protected by a moat that was 50 feet (15.24 m) wide and 5 feet (1.5 m) deep in parts. Its earthen walls rose 30 feet (9.1 m) in the air and extended over 600 feet (183 m) from east to west and a little under 300 feet (91.4 m) from north to south. The narrow stretch of beach approaching Wagner was approximately 100 yards (91.4 m) wide bordered by a marshy swamp to the west and the Atlantic Ocean to the east.

Prior to the arrival of the 54th Regiment to Morris Island, General Quincy Adams Gillmore had been tasked with leading the attack on Charleston, the birthplace of the rebellion. His plan was to take control of Morris Island, place heavy artillery at Cummings Point, the northern tip of Morris Island less than 1,500 yards (1,371.6 m) away from Fort Sumter. After securing Morris Island, Gillmore planned to blanket Fort Sumter with heavy fire. This would weaken the Confederate occupation to the point that the army and naval forces could quickly seize Charleston.

Gillmore, along with Union forces, landed on southern Morris Island early on July 10th, 1863, and swiftly progressed northward, overwhelming Confederate troops on their trek to the southern wall of Wagner. Gillmore hoped to take Morris by the next day and sent three regiments to rush Wagner at

If you look closely at this painting of the 54th Regiment's attack on Fort Wagner, you can see that the artist depicted the moment that Colonel Shaw was mortally wounded.

first light on July 11th. The Confederate defenders drove the Union soldiers back, exacting 339 casualties. Gillmore was forced to regroup and decided to attack again. This time, he planned to execute a coordinated bombardment from both land and sea. After the bombardment, Gillmore intended to send around 5,000 Union soldiers up the beach to secure the island. Union forces began firing on Wagner on the morning of July 18th. The onslaught lasted longer than eight hours, and more than nine thousand shells were fired, leading Union soldiers to believe that Confederate forces had sustained mass casualties. In fact, only 8 of the 1,620 soldiers occupying Wagner had been killed. At 7:45 pm that evening, ignorant of the lack of damage the bombardment had caused, the Union forces advanced to the north under the eerie light of the setting sun. They were led by the 54th Regiment of Massachusetts.

Colonel Shaw led the charge, marching beside the flag bearer in the first line as the regiment made its way up the narrow beach. The beach offered no cover, and the soldiers' advance was quick. As Wagner grew closer, Colonel Shaw ordered his men to approach at a jogging pace. The beach continued to narrow as the Union army closed in on Wagner. Sandwiched between with the unnavigable marsh to the west and the Atlantic Ocean to the east, the men fell into a V-shaped formation with the colonel and the US flag at the helm. As the Union army moved swiftly towards the Confederate stronghold, Colonel Shaw raised his sword and ordered his men to charge. The bayonets of the 54th Regiment were lowered as their legs carried them quickly into battle.

Confederate forces fired on their assailants as they came within 100 yards (91.4 m) of Wagner. The 54th rushed headlong into danger, and they soon discovered that they had underestimated the Confederate defenders. The 54th had been assured by General Strong that they were facing possibly 300 soldiers, but nearly six times that many Confederate soldiers remained in defense of Wagner. Casualties were numerous and immediate.

Blue and gray uniforms littered the shore as projectiles whizzed through the air and through the bodies of Union soldiers. Nevertheless, Colonel Shaw led his men to the walls of Wagner and managed to reach the **parapet** of the earthen fort before being struck through the heart. The injury proved fatal, yet just before he fell, Colonel Shaw urged his men onward into the Confederate stronghold.

As the battle raged, twenty-three-year-old Sergeant William H. Carney took the national flag that Shaw had been carrying, made his way up the parapet and planted it. The 54th held their station for almost an hour. Though Carney sustained four wounds in the legs, chest, and arm, he was able to keep the flag planted until reinforcements arrived, allowing the badly battered 54th Regiment to withdraw. While his multiple wounds forced Carney's discharge from the 54th, he was awarded the Congressional Medal of Honor in May of 1900, the first African American ever to be recognized with the highest military decoration.

The 54th began their approach of Fort Wagner at dusk and the battle was over by 1:00 am. Though the tide had been low when they set out, it had risen and the dead were bathed with

Robert Smalls

While the 54th Regiment of Massachusetts fought valiantly on land, black sailors served on the seas. One African American refused to be held by the bonds of slavery and not only freed himself and several other slaves but also provided supplies to the Union army in one courageous undertaking.

Robert Smalls was a twenty-three-year-old slave from Beaufort, South Carolina, who had been pressed into service on a Confederate warship named *The Planter*. For more than a year, Smalls observed the movements and signals of the Confederate sailors. In the spring of 1862, the Union successfully captured Port Royal and occupied the area just a few miles away from the Charleston Harbor, where Smalls and *The Planter* were stationed. On May 13th, 1862, while his white shipmates attended a gala on land, Smalls seized his opportunity. He and the other slaves aboard *The Planter* picked up their families at a nearby wharf then turned *The Planter* around and began to sail past Confederate checkpoints with the Confederate flag raised to avoid suspicion.

Dressed in the captain's straw hat and jacket, Smalls mimicked the captain's walk and upon passing each fort gave the correct signal to Confederate watchmen. Smalls effectively disguised himself past each fort and lowered the Confederate flag, raising a white flag in its place once the ship reached open

Robert Smalls freed his crew, his family, and himself while delivering a Confederate ship to Union forces and went on to serve in the US House of Representatives.

waters. The Union troops were astonished and grateful. Not only had Smalls managed to deliver a Confederate warship, *The Planter* also carried two hundred pounds of ammunition and four big guns that were now available for Union use.

seawater while some of the wounded drowned. Ultimately, the 54th lost their beloved Colonel Robert Gould Shaw; 272 other men of their regiment were killed, wounded, or missing. Altogether, the 54th Regiment of Massachusetts was reduced by 42 percent with 1,515 total Union casualties compared to only 174 Confederate casualties. Though the second assault on Fort Sumter was unsuccessful, the courage and honor of black soldiers had been undoubtedly proven by the actions of the 54th Regiment of Massachusetts.

THE BATTLE OF OLUSTEE

In February of 1864, the now-famous 54th Regiment of Massachusetts was dispatched to Florida to fight in the battle of Olustee. The Union was interested in securing Florida both politically and militarily. Though Florida was technically part of the Confederacy, it was scarcely inhabited and most rebel troops were elsewhere, fighting for territory that was more vital to their cause. Union troops were sent to Jacksonville on February 7th and continued to push inland. President Lincoln's private secretary, John Hay, followed troops and issued loyalty oaths to residents in an attempt to create a new state government that could then send delegates to the 1864 Republican Party convention. The Union also had an interest in disturbing Confederate supply routes that ran through Florida and in acquiring more black recruits.

On February 20th, 1864, a battle between Confederate and Union armies raged for almost five hours near Ocean Pond in Olustee, Florida. Each opposing commander deployed their troops gradually, but the Confederate soldiers were able to establish a more advantageous position. The 54th marched

The 54th Regiment are said to have marched into Olustee shouting, "Three cheers for Massachusetts and seven dollars a month." This was meant to boost the morale of black soldiers who were still receiving less pay than whites.

from the rear of the Union advance and saw evidence of a slaughter as they approached the battlefield. Upon arrival in the combat zone, the 54th fought as reinforcements for soldiers that were already deeply embroiled in battle and provided enough cover fire to allow a safe retreat. The 54th Regiment of Massachusetts had once again traveled a great distance to fight valiantly. They had marched 110 miles (177 km) in 100 hours before they reached the battlefield and provided relief for Union forces at Olustee prior to making their own retreat. An estimated 1,860 Union soldiers were killed, wounded, or missing; Florida remained under Confederate control for the remainder of the war.

Safe from imminent danger, surviving Union troops still had the long journey back to Jacksonville ahead of them. Along the way, the 54th Regiment was ordered to march back in the opposite direction to assist with a locomotive that had broken down carrying wounded soldiers. The soldiers marched back to the train, attached ropes and pulled it to the next station.

WITNESS, PROTEST, AND DEDICATED SERVICE

Members of the 54th Regiment of Massachusetts fought in Georgia, South Carolina, and Florida. They helped change public opinion about black service members' military contributions. They achieved this not only with their incredible service but also with an organized, concentrated protest. Their determined fight for justice in this country and their performance in battle continues to serve as a model of patriotism and military excellence.

LEGACY OF THE 54TH REGIMENT OF MASSACHUSETTS

Like other soldiers, men of the 54th penned letters home to their families and loved ones, but they also served as war correspondents and wrote to news publications detailing their experiences. These published accounts helped the case for black armed forces in the same way that Harriet Beecher Stowe's novel *Uncle Tom's Cabin* had softened white attitudes towards the plight of enslaved blacks. Reading the accounts of these soldiers helped white people to learn about Civil War conflicts through the eyes of the very soldiers that were engaged in them, soldiers that many had assumed were not up to the task of military service. Written accounts like that of Frederick Douglass's son Lewis illuminated the horrors of battle and the mettle of those who managed to survive.

Stand Watie

While many of the events leading up to the Civil War concerned the plight of black Americans and their search for freedom, another group faced an uncertain future. As a result of the **Indian Removal Act** signed by Andrew Jackson on May 28th, 1830, many Native Americans had been forcibly removed from their lands by factions empowered by the government. The Cherokee Nation was one of the most affected groups of this disenfranchising act. Dissent within the tribe regarding whether or not to peaceably relocate led to turmoil among the Cherokee people. Not only were they eventually forcibly removed, but the split Nation descended into chaos as those that were for the relocation took murderous revenge on those that had resisted the forced migration. One Cherokee man would rise from this disorder to become one of the most successful Confederate officers to serve in the American Civil War.

Opposite: Though he is less famous than his white counterparts, Stand Watie was one of the most dedicated and successful generals that served in the Civil War.

AMERICAN GREED

In the late 1820s, white **prospectors** rushed to what is now the state of Georgia in the hopes of discovering gold. The land had belonged to the Cherokee Nation but, as more and more whites flooded the area, resentment for the Native Americans already inhabiting the land grew. Though the land was rightfully

White settlers often clashed with natives as a result of white prospectors illegally mining on native grounds as this image illustrates.

owned by the Cherokee Nation per federal treaties, Georgia confiscated much of the land, and soon the federal government intervened. The government's solution was to move the Native Americans west to what is now Oklahoma, freeing their land up for white settlers. The Indian Removal Act empowered the government to offer money and land in exchange for Native American migration. Enormous pressure was exerted on tribes to sign treaties and abandon their homes. The decision of whether to accept the government's terms and leave or refuse to move weighed heavily on the Cherokee people and split the group into two camps. While most Cherokees believed they had a right to remain on their land, others believed that their people had a better chance of maintaining their independence if they complied with federal terms. In 1835, the Treaty of New Echota was supported and signed by the minority of Cherokees who believed the tribe's survival was contingent upon submission to government demands. Stand Watie and his family were among those that signed and advocated for removal. Some of the Cherokees, including the Waties, made the journey West in 1837 to land referred to as Indian Territory while others refused to leave.

The faction who resisted migration was led by Cherokee leader John Ross, Stand Watie's most notable adversary. In 1839, those Cherokees and other Native Americans, freedmen, and enslaved blacks who had remained were forced from their homes and made to relocate to Indian Territory by militia empowered by the federal government. Though the death toll is impossible to pinpoint, it is estimated that, of around fifteen thousand Cherokee that made the journey, around four thousand died on what became known as the Trail of Tears.

Once Cherokees arrived in Indian Territory, they found those that had supported the relocation had secured the most desirable tracts of land. Those that had resisted removal sought revenge on the other Cherokee faction whom they felt were responsible for the loss of their homes and loved ones. Those that refused to sign the treaty invoked the Blood Law. This provision stated that anyone who separated tribal lands from the tribe was subject to the death penalty. Immediately, the opposing Cherokees began warring with each other, committing brutal assassinations without mercy. Watie's brother, uncle, and cousin were executed, though Stand Watie himself managed to escape this fate. The Cherokee experienced their own civil war for years. In 1842, Stand Watie crossed paths with one of his uncle's assassins and shot him. He was tried for murder but ultimately found not guilty for reasons of self-defense, even though his uncle's assailant had been unarmed. It is estimated that the Cherokee Nation experienced around thirty-five political assassinations between 1845 and 1846.

AN OPPORTUNITY FOR ORDER

When the Civil War broke out in 1861, the Cherokees were faced with another governmental choice. While Union forces were less interested in recruiting Native Americans at the war's outset, Confederate forces courted the Cherokee with promises of payment, land, and even governmental office if they helped the South to victory. Stand Watie, who had built a successful plantation on Indian Territory and was himself a slave owner, was enticed by the Confederacy's offers. Not only was he interested in maintaining his ability to own slaves, but the promise of being a recognized citizen and starting over with a new government that had not cheated or endangered his people pushed him to side with the rebellion. John Ross, Watie's old rival, supported the Union and spent the Civil War in Washington lobbying for the Cherokee people. Though Watie's troops were ill-equipped, they were resourceful and carried out merciless guerilla warfare on horseback. Under Watie's command, they used concealment tactics and survivalist skills to frustrate the Union army throughout the war.

SECURING INDIAN TERRITORY

The Confederacy had a vested interest in securing Indian Territory as it helped to stem the flow of Union soldiers to various battles, and it was also used by Union forces to send supplies to troops. Stand Watie and his men became experts

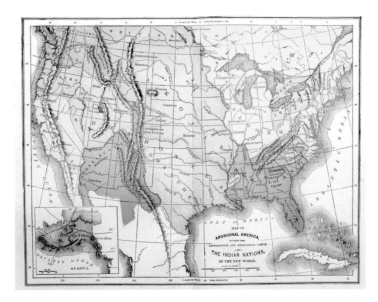

While native tribes were established across the United States, many were relocated to an area known as Indian Territory, most of which is now Oklahoma.

at drawing Union troops away from the vital theaters of war along the Eastern Seaboard and the inland Southeast. After performing admirably in the bloody Battle of Wilson's Creek, Watie was promoted to colonel, and along with his regiment, the 2nd Cherokee Mounted Rifles, he spent the war reinforcing Confederates, attacking Union troops in Indian Territory, and disrupting Union supply lines. More than ninety battles were waged in Indian Territory as Confederates attempted to draw Union troops from the East.

Another Missouri conflict, the Battle of Pea Ridge, cemented Watie's reputation as an invaluable Confederate asset. While the Confederacy experienced around 4,600 casualties and suffered a resounding defeat, Watie had managed to capture a Union battery in the midst of the bloodbath. Watie knew the Union army was better equipped and better trained. Watie's decision to attack Union supply lines was both tactically sound and necessary in order for his troops to continue with adequate supplies. The mounted Cherokees undertook hit-and-run attacks on any Union troops that strayed from forts located in Indian Territory. The Cherokees were able to conceal themselves even in broad daylight, partly because they dressed as Federal soldiers. By presenting themselves as allies to Union soldiers, they found a way to carry out surprise attacks and attain adequate supplies.

As Confederate forces waged major battles in the East, Stand Watie intensified his attacks against Union troops attempting to relocate along the Kansas border. These attacks frustrated the Union, and eventually Union commanders had no choice but to make Stand Watie's capture a priority. His persistent assaults along with his ability to conceal himself and evade capture were covered by the American press. Newspapers begin to refer to him as "The Red Fox."

Stand Watie terrorized both Union forces and sympathizers in the Indian Territory, raiding and burning the land of those that lived in the area but supported the North. Many of these homes and tracts of land belonged to fellow Native Americans. Watie was staunch in his support of the Confederacy and spent the war doing everything in his power to ensure a Southern victory.

THE AMBUSH OF STEAMBOAT *J. R. WILLIAMS*

As a result of Confederate losses at Fort Smith and the First Battle at Cabin Creek, the Union army enjoyed exclusive control of the Arkansas River. This allowed them an alternate route to supply troops further south. Prior to controlling the waterway, Union supplies had traveled south via wagon trains, which were susceptible to Confederate ambush. The Arkansas River offered a safer, more effective way to deliver food and munitions without risking an attack from the Confederate army, or so they thought.

On June 15, 1864, as the steamboat *J. R. Williams* made its way up the river, it rounded a bend at Pleasant Bluff where a force of four hundred Confederate soldiers open fired with small arms and canons. The boat was disabled by the heavy fire. Though the Union crew was able to run the boat aground on the bank of the river opposite the Confederate threat, they soon realized they were vastly outnumbered and overwhelmed. The men abandoned ship and fled to a nearby Union camp, where they notified others of the ambush. Watie and his men boarded the ship, towed it to a sand bar, and began loading as much of the steamboat's bounty onto their horses as possible. Many of the Confederate soldiers made off with their wares once the ship had been raided, abandoning Watie. Later that day, Union reinforcements arrived and fired on the Confederacy, but Watie managed to set the steamboat on fire and withdraw from the engagement with his remaining men.

While the ambush of the *J. R. Williams* did not have much effect on the outcome of the Civil War, it served as a morale boost for the Confederate army and holds a unique distinction of being the only naval battle fought in what is now Oklahoma. The cargo aboard the vessel is said to have been worth around $120,000. Though the steamboat's ambush was an important point in Watie's military career, his plunder was nothing compared to what he would successfully secure in his next attack.

THE SECOND BATTLE OF CABIN CREEK

In the summer of 1864, after being promoted to Brigadier General, Stand Watie received information from a prisoner of war regarding a large shipment of Union supplies. A wagon train traveling from Fort Scott, in modern-day Kansas, to Fort Gibson, situated in what is now Oklahoma, was said to be carrying a million dollars' worth of supplies. The three hundred wagons carting supplies to three thousand troops and nine thousand refugees presented an opportunity for Watie and his resourceful men. Aware of the route the wagons would take and the lay of the land, Watie contacted fellow Confederate General Richard Gano. Together they gathered some two thousand troops made up of both white and Native American soldiers and began planning the attack.

On September 18, 1864, the two commanders assembled their troops on the bluffs along Cabin Creek and waited for nightfall. While the 450 Union soldiers guarding the camp slept, the Confederate troops approached. Richard Gano

Union wagon trains like the one featured here transported supplies, food, and troops across Confederate lines and often were targeted by Stand Watie and his troops.

Ely S. Parker

Ely S. Parker, a member of the Seneca tribe, was a civil engineer who also had a law degree. When Lincoln issued a call for recruits, Parker jumped at the chance to serve his country. Other educated men immediately became officers, but Parker was denied the opportunity to serve at all.

He offered to raise a regiment of volunteer Iroquois and was refused. He later attempted to offer his talents as an engineer but was again turned away. Secretary of State William Seward informed him, "The fight must be settled by the white men alone. Go home, cultivate your farm, and we will settle our troubles without any Indian aid."

In the years leading up to the Civil War, Parker had spent his time learning the science of engineering firsthand. He worked on the extension of the Genesee Valley Canal in the 1850s and began to oversee more and more constructions as the years progressed. During his time in Galena, Illinois, Parker became friends with a frustrated former US army officer who was working as a local store clerk. That store clerk was Ulysses S. Grant, the man who would become the leader of the Union army.

In 1863, Grant was able to fulfill Parker's wish of serving for the Union army. Parker began his military career with the US army in Brig. Gen. J. E. Smith's division in Vicksburg,

Ely S. Parker was an attorney and an engineer before serving in the Union army, eventually becoming General Ulysses S. Grant's personal military secretary.

Mississippi. He quickly rose through the ranks. By 1864, he was selected to serve as Grant's personal military secretary.

Ely Parker's most famed act in the Civil War was the drafting of the terms of Confederate surrender at Appomattox. It is said that General Robert E. Lee greeted Parker by saying, "I am glad to see one real American here," to which Ely S. Parker replied, "We are all Americans."

and his men advanced from the east while Watie brought his troops in from the west. The creek itself offered a third flank, effectively cornering the unsuspecting Union soldiers. As the stars shone and the Northern troops slept, the Confederates fired. They did not attack the soldiers directly but opted to shoot the mules used to pull the wagons. Though they had been quietly grazing seconds earlier, the shots sent the mules into a stampede through the Union camp, awaking the soldiers to a disorienting chaos. The shocked Union forces were immediately overwhelmed and had no option but to flee. One hundred and sixty Union troops were wounded while only forty-five Confederates sustained injuries from the attack. Watie and his men loaded up what provisions they could and burned the rest. Though Union reinforcements were sent to from Fort Gibson, the Confederate soldiers eluded capture.

The fact that munitions and supplies needed to continue the Union war effort were stolen unnerved the Union and inspired the Confederacy. News of the successful raid traveled all the way to Jefferson Davis's office just as Confederate forces were drawn away from Indian Territory. In the East, William Tecumseh Sherman had reached Atlanta. Despite Watie's best efforts, the Confederacy was on the precipice of defeat.

WATIE STANDS FIRM

At birth, Stand Watie was given the Cherokee name Degataga, which means "stand firm." As the war came to a close, Watie lived up to his name. A die-hard Confederate who spent his military service raiding Union supplies and wreaking havoc on Northern supporters in Indian Territory, Watie was confident of a Confederate victory. When news of Lee's surrender at

Appomattox reached the Cherokee general, he was in utter disbelief. While the Confederacy experienced heavy losses in the East, Watie had seen mostly victory in the Indian Territory. On June 23rd, 1865, Stand Watie finally laid down his arms, ending his military career a full seventy-five days after Lee signed the terms of surrender.

A CONTROVERSIAL FIGURE DESTROYED

Although Watie fought skillfully and admirably, he fought for the losing side of the Civil War. The Cherokee Nation sent delegations to represent both the Union Cherokee and the Southern Cherokee. Watie served as the Southern Cherokee delegate and lobbied for the recognition of a separate Southern Cherokee Nation. The United States government refused but did negotiate with the Union Cherokee represented by Watie's old rival, John Ross. Ross was declared the principal chief but died shortly after and a new chief was appointed in his stead.

Upon surrender, Watie returned to his home to find it had been burned to the ground by Union soldiers. In the years following the Civil War, Watie would see the government take large tracts of land from the Cherokee as punishment for their Confederate support. This land was then distributed to other tribes. He found himself in desperate financial ruin and spent his last years farming. He lived to see the deaths of all his sons and died himself in 1871.

BROTHER AGAINST BROTHER

While the Civil War was a shock to Americans who had not seen internal violence on a widespread scale, the Cherokee Nation had grown quite accustomed to civil chaos by the time

John Ross was the Cherokee Nation's principal chief directly after the Civil War. He was also Stand Watie's rival.

America descended into war. The Civil War left the Cherokee Nation weakened: with both of its old leaders dead and a new chief, the Cherokees were thrust into **Reconstruction** era and went back to being seen as a nuisance and an obstacle to white settlers.

Native Americans fought for both sides of the war but none was more notable nor achieved the military success and rank that Stand Watie had. Yet Watie is still a controversial figure today. He waged war on his own people, actively supporting the rebel forces and holding slaves. Nevertheless, Watie's courageous and ingenious resistance is remembered, despite the war's outcome.

A Hero's Welcome?

After Robert E. Lee's surrender to Ulysses S. Grant at
Appomattox Courthouse, the era of Reconstruction
began. While black veterans hoped that their service
proved them worthy of the same opportunities as white men,
the United States government would enact a variety of policies
that dashed those dreams.

Reconstruction was marked by political battling, racial
prejudice, and continued violence in the South. Though black
Americans were able to make some gains, opportunities for
advancement were few and far between. Reconstruction
would last just over ten years and end as a result of Southern
resentment and Northern exhaustion.

VICTORY MARCH

Once the Civil War was officially over, black troops led the
march on Charleston, South Carolina, where the war had begun

Opposite: At war's end, soldiers and freedmen marched through the
streets celebrating the Union victory. Here a procession through the
streets of Charleston, South Carolina, features freedmen alongside
the 55th African American Massachusetts Regiment.

four years prior. The 21st U.S. Colored Infantry marched in first, followed by soldiers from the 54th Regiment of Massachusetts. Black residents crowded the streets, cheering on the black soldiers and rejoicing in shared victory while white residents stayed indoors. Black veterans were greeted with a resounding hero's welcome by black citizens—both those who had never known slavery and the newly emancipated.

Many former slaves were notified of the war's end by black soldiers who offered a dignified example of the possibilities of freedom. They expected respect and fair treatment from white people and set about liberating slaves whose masters had ignored the Emancipation Proclamation. Soldiers counseled the newly freed blacks on how to air their grievances to appropriate officials, even though these grievances were almost never given official consideration.

VETERANS HONORED

Eighteen black soldiers who had fought in the Civil War were awarded the Medal of Honor. However, some recipients were not decorated until long after their service. By the end of 1865, thirteen black soldiers had been recognized for their contribution to the Union army; all but one was honored for fighting in the Battle of New Market Heights. Five years later, a soldier from the same battle was honored, and another four years after that. William H. Carney, the noble soldier with the 54th Regiment at Fort Wagner, was finally recognized with the Medal of Honor in 1900, thirty-five years after the war had ended. He died eight years later. The final two recipients were honored in 1914 and 2001, respectively. Though they had composed about 10 percent of the Union army and numbered around 179,000, only eighteen black veterans have been recognized for military excellence by the United States government for their service during the Civil War.

RECLAIMING WHAT WAS LOST

Once the celebrations ended, black veterans set about reclaiming all that they had lost during the war and the years preceding the conflict. They were engaged in the nearly impossible task of locating loved ones who had been separated from them at auction. Ads began appearing in newspapers all over the country with descriptions of loved ones and information on where and when they were last seen. Though some were reunited, many went unfound.

Black veterans also assisted in lobbying the government for the protection of black residents where they were being persecuted. Calvin Holly was a black soldier posted in Vicksburg, Mississippi, who witnessed terrible violence against African Americans living in the city. He contacted government officials informing them of newly freed residents being left to starve and freeze to death, hoping that the government would pass laws protecting black citizens.

Lost Friends.

NOTE.—We receive many letters asking for information about lost friends. All such letters will be published in this column. We make no charge for publishing these letters from subscribers to the SOUTHWESTERN. All others will please enclose fifty cents to pay for publishing the notices. Pastors will please read the requests published below from their pulpits, and report any case where friends are brought together by means of letters in the SOUTHWESTERN.

DEAR EDITOR—I wish to inquire about my people. I left them in a trader's yard in Alexandria, with a Mr. Franklin. They were to be sent to New Orleans. Their names were Jarvis, Moses, George and Maria Gains. Any information of them will be thankfully received. Address me at Aberdeen, Miss.
CELIA RHODES.

Newspapers were filled with ads like this one, placed by friends and relatives who had been separated from their loved ones by slavery.

Veterans also helped establish communities by organizing and building schools and churches. Soldiers from the Third Colored Arkansas Volunteers constructed an orphanage in Helena, Arkansas. Others rebuilt homes and helped establish farms on large tracts of land shared by black families.

FINDING WORK

When the war ended, black veterans were faced with the task of securing employment. Discrimination and lack of experience forced many veterans to take jobs that paid menial wages, similar to those they had held before the war. Most veterans dreamed of owning land and some did, though they were forced to either pool their money with other black families or spend the entirety of their military salary on a land purchase.

Although some veterans sought to build a steady civilian life, thousands wanted to remain in the armed forces. Congress was happy to oblige these soldiers and created six black regiments meant to serve as permanent fixtures in the United States army. These regiments were commanded by white officers and paid the same as white soldiers. Though the pay was not much, it was steady. Around 12,500 men volunteered for service, most of them Civil War veterans.

The regiments were eventually expanded and reorganized. Two regiments, the 24th and 25th Infantry Regiments, helped settle violence related to land ownership along the US-Mexico border. The other two regiments were the Ninth and Tenth cavalries. The cavalries rode through the West engaging in battles between settlers who believed they had a right to Western land and Native Americans who had inhabited the land before whites arrived. The black troops were soon referred to as Buffalo Soldiers.

THE DEATH OF AN AMERICAN LEADER

Though the tasks of Reconstruction were daunting, many Americans had great faith in the man who had led them through the bloodiest conflict in history to lead them forward towards reconciliation. Unfortunately, this would not come to pass. Five days after Lee's surrender and the official end of the four-year Civil War, Lincoln was killed. He was shot in the back of the head as he watched a play at Ford's Theatre in Washington, DC. His assassin was John Wilkes Booth, a well-known actor and Confederate sympathizer. Though Booth evaded capture on the night of the killing, he was eventually located, shot, and killed.

The same citizens who had rejoiced at the end of the war were now reeling with grief and rage. Though Booth saw swift justice after an extensive manhunt, the country was in upheaval. With Lincoln dead, the United States would have to depend on his successor, Andrew Johnson, to navigate Reconstruction.

A NEW PRESIDENT

Andrew Johnson took the presidency at a time of immense turmoil. The country had just finished fighting the bloodiest war in its history and the South was decimated. Four million newly liberated Americans were without homes, work, or education; white Southern families had been devastated by the war both through violence and the destruction of property.

President Johnson believed black people to be inferior to whites and had little to no interest in clarifying or protecting their rights. However, Johnson also held wealthy Southern planters in contempt. Johnson identified with poor whites in the South and sought to ensure that impoverished blacks would not infringe on jobs or land that he saw as the birthright of whites.

He would work to limit black freedom throughout Reconstruction, warring with **Radical Republicans**, a segment of the Republican Party that passionately supported the rights of freedmen.

THE STRUGGLE TO BECOME CITIZENS

Though the end of the Civil War saw the abolishment of the system of slavery in the United States, there was still the question of what to do with the millions of newly freed slaves that many referred to as freedmen. Cotton was still the number one export of the United States and both Northerners and Southerners wanted to continue to profit from the cash crop. However, without legal human bondage, workers would have to be paid. The more frightening reality was the possibility that the freedmen might refuse to work the fields at all, potentially bringing about an economic collapse.

White Americans wrestled with the idea those they treated as inferior subordinates were no longer obligated to serve their purposes. Alternatively, black people were wrestling with what freedom meant and how to make the most of it.

The Freedmen's Bureau

Two months before Lee's surrender at Appomattox, the federal government established the United States Bureau of Refugees, Freedmen and Abandoned Lands (commonly known as the **Freedmen's Bureau**). The bureau was established to help newly

The Freedmen's Bureau was developed to settle disputes between newly freed African Americans and white civilians.

freed blacks transition into American society. Without enough funding or staffing and mired in political resistance, the bureau struggled to carry out the myriad social tasks it was responsible for. The bureau employed only nine hundred agents across the eleven formerly Confederate states, and often the agents were subject to violent uprisings from Southern whites who felt they were meddling in Southern affairs. President Johnson seemed to agree. At times, corruption plagued the bureau.

Though the Freedmen's Bureau was hindered by politics and violence, its agents managed to assist the black community, and the South, in a variety of ways. They built hospitals and helped black citizens negotiate labor contracts. They also helped to settle labor disputes, though they often sided with white citizens. Agents worked to obtain marriage licenses for former slaves and even assisted freedmen with locating their loved ones.

Perhaps one of the most important contributions of the Freedmen's Bureau was the education of black Americans. The bureau built thousands of schools for newly freed black Americans who were anxious to educate themselves. It helped establish several schools that are now considered historically black colleges and universities, such as Howard University, Fisk University, and Hampton University.

In 1872, Congress bowed to pressure from white Southerners who were tired of what they considered Northern interference. Northerners were exhausted from the war and ambivalent about the rights and struggles of black Americans. The Freedmen's Bureau was dismantled after only seven years of service, leaving black people in America to fend for themselves.

Special Field Order #15

Shortly after reaching Savannah, General William Tecumseh Sherman declared that freedmen would receive land under **Special Field Order #15**. Issued on January 16th, 1865, this directive set aside a tract of land stretching 245 miles (394.3 km) along the Southeast coast from Charleston to Jacksonville. The head of each family received a "possessory title," which entitled them to 40 acres (16.2 hectares). Sherman also allowed the use of army mules for working the land, thus the phrase "Forty acres and a mule."

The lands set aside for black inhabitants included the Sea Islands. St. Catherine's, an island on the coast of Georgia, became a safe haven and home for newly freed men. A man named Tunis Campbell was commissioned to oversee the resettlement. Campbell set about building schools, farming, and easing the people into life after the horrors of slavery.

He requested seed, plows, tools, and other necessities from the United States government and set up a government for Sea Island as well.

Eventually, Southern whites began to return to the land they had abandoned during the war in an attempt to reclaim what they saw as theirs. When one such man returned to the Sea Islands, the newly formed Sea Islands Congress passed a law that no white person could step foot on their territory.

Sadly, Special Order #15 was not honored in the end. Andrew Johnson sided with the planters and began pardoning thousands of former Confederates. The land that was already distributed per Sherman's order was to be returned to its prewar owners. Though some Southern whites offered labor contracts, allowing African Americans to remain on their land as long as they received a generous portion of the profits (known as **sharecropping**), most freedmen wanted lives that were separate from those they used to serve. In an unfortunate twist of fate, a large company of black soldiers was sent to St. Catherine's with the express purpose of returning the land to its previous owner. Though the freedmen were willing to engage in conflict with white people, they had no desire to attack black soldiers. The freedmen on St. Catherine's Island dispersed and went in search of opportunity elsewhere.

Resulting Amendments

Amendments to the Constitution provided the possibility of lasting change for many black Americans. While proclamations and pieces of legislature were encouraging, changes to the Constitution ultimately signified that African Americans were recognized members of society.

The **Thirteenth Amendment** was the first to change the lives of black Americans; it was passed on January 31st, 1865. The Thirteenth Amendment prohibited slavery in the United States. The language of the amendment reads, "Neither slavery nor involuntary servitude, except as a punishment for crime whereof the party shall have been duly convicted, shall exist within the United States, or any place subject to their jurisdiction." While the amendment's passage was encouraging, Southern state legislatures would use the loophole of criminal punishment to reinstate the exploitation of black labor.

The **Fourteenth Amendment** passed on July 9th, 1868, and guaranteed citizenship to anyone born in the United States. This amendment helped clarify the position of freedmen in America and brought them a step closer to having the same rights as other United States citizens.

Finally, the **Fifteenth Amendment** was ratified on February 3rd, 1870. This amendment was terrifying to many white people and immensely important to African Americans because it guaranteed them suffrage, or the right to vote. Black Americans hoped that the ability to participate in electing public officials would give them more agency and control over their lives.

Criminalizing Black Life

In late 1865, after the passage of the Thirteenth Amendment, Southern states scrambled for a way to ensure that black subservience would continue to be the law of the land. Southern whites were concerned that their access to free labor would disappear, a horrifying thought to them in an already decimated economy. Though the Thirteenth Amendment had abolished slavery, there was an exception. Involuntary servitude was legal if it served as criminal punishment. As a means of trying to create a system that was as close to slavery as possible, southern states began passing laws that restricted black freedom. These laws became known as **black codes**.

Black codes made a wide variety of actions illegal for black Americans. For example, it was a crime for blacks to speak loudly in front of a group of white women, there were laws that instituted a curfew, laws that made it a crime to be unemployed (**vagrancy laws**), and laws that made it a crime to own weapons. There were laws called **apprentice laws** that allowed black children to be taken if white officials deemed them neglected or mistreated. While these laws were almost exclusively applied to African Americans, there was also legislation that criminalized white support of black people. There were harsher penalties enforced for interracial relations and **antienticement laws** that made it a crime to offer a black person a job or better wages if they were already employed.

Pig laws focused on increased penalties for theft of livestock and tools of the field. Though these acts were criminal before the pig laws, they were now felonies and the convicted were subject to lengthy jail sentences. Often African Americans were falsely accused of theft when in fact they were entitled to livestock or other items as a means of payment. The result of these laws was a change in the prison population that occurred almost overnight. Suddenly Southern jails were filled with black bodies and the association of black people with criminal behavior became the norm.

Inadequate space and insufficient funds to feed prisoners posed a significant dilemma for Southern lawmakers. As a solution, many states began convict leasing, loaning out prisoners to private companies for labor. Companies paid a small fee to lease convicts and were responsible for their housing and feeding. The state made a profit and corporations benefitted from incredibly cheap labor performed by people without the ability to protest.

Though the Emancipation Proclamation and the Thirteenth Amendment went a long way toward ending slave labor, the Southern state legislatures found ways to circumvent the will of the federal government. They were able to bring about a new system of forced labor that would remain in place for decades to come.

VIOLENCE CONTINUES

While the age of Reconstruction brought about the birth of black freedom in the United States, it also ushered in a new brand of racial violence. White Southerners resented the presence of Freedmen's Bureau agents in their cities. They were infuriated by the sight of black people, whom they used to control, now walking down the same streets as they did. Some decided to take the matter of subduing the black population into their own hands.

While attacks on African Americans were nothing new, several organizations modeled after slavecatching patrols began to use violent coercion as a systematic method of limiting black people's freedoms. The most famous of these groups was the Ku Klux Klan.

Originally formed in 1866, the Klan spread quickly throughout the South, with members in almost every formerly Confederate state by 1870. Klansmen rode on horseback in

In the aftermath of the Civil War, organizations aimed at racial terrorism were established throughout the south, the most famous of which survives to this day: the Ku Klux Klan.

small groups and terrorized black citizens. They targeted black politicians, black people who owned property, black people that were seen as an inspiration to other blacks, and white sympathizers who aided black Americans. The Klan dragged freedmen from their beds and harassed pedestrians who were unlucky enough to be found walking after dark. The Klan stabbed, whipped, and burned their victims—sometimes killing them.

The goal of the KKK was to suppress the black population in any way they could. Specifically, they aimed to intimidate black people into giving up political office and scare would-be voters from exercising their rights. Their crimes were hard to prosecute because of the group's secret membership and the silent approval of many Southern whites; witnesses willing

Buffalo Soldiers

After the Civil War ended, some black soldiers wished to remain in the armed forces. Some had grown accustomed to military life; others thought they'd have a better chance at equality in the armed forces than they did living as civilians. In 1866, when the United States government began recruiting men for its black regiments, black soldiers who enlisted agreed to serve for five years and were paid $13 every month. With an offer of more money than they could ever hope to make outside of military service, Civil War veterans enthusiastically signed on.

The duties of these cavalry and infantry units ranged from protecting white settlers as they relocated westward to battling the Apache natives. The nickname "Buffalo Soldiers" has stuck throughout history, but whether or not it was a term of respect used by Native Americans is debated. Some believe they were referred to this way for racist reasons: because of their curly, coarse hair or their black skin. Another theory is that they fought hard like the buffalo and thus the comparison was made. Some think that they were called Buffalo Soldiers simply because they wore large coats made of buffalo hide as they rode through the winter.

While the United States government used the Buffalo Soldiers in part to subdue Native Americans and allow whites to take their lands, the soldiers showed the same courage and discipline that they had in the Civil War. They had the lowest

After the Civil War ended, the government recruited soldiers for black regiments who would come to be known as Buffalo Soldiers.

desertion and court-martial rates in the entire army. Fourteen of the Buffalo Soldiers earned the Medal of Honor between the years of 1870 and 1890. Several more would enjoy the same recognition after fighting in successive conflicts.

to speak out were hard to come by. Eventually, the rampant violence caused Congress to intervene. The Ku Klux Klan Act made it a federal crime for individuals to conspire to deny citizens the right to hold office and serve on juries. The act also extended authority to the federal government to arrest those accused without charge. This extension of power enraged Democrats and even some Republicans who saw the act as the federal government overstepping its boundaries. Despite the legislation, the Ku Klux Klan survived Reconstruction and still has thousands of active members in the deep South today.

RECONSTRUCTION ENDS

In 1877, amid bitter fighting between politicians and continued horrific violence in the South, Reconstruction came to a close just twelve years after the Civil War ended. The presidential election of 1876 between Democrat Samuel Tilden and Republican Rutherford B. Hayes had been bitterly contested. Democrats offered to accept Hayes as their president under the condition that the Republicans would end Reconstruction and leave the South to sort out its own conflicts. Republicans agreed, and this informal deal to end Reconstruction became known as the **Compromise of 1877**. Federal troops were withdrawn from Southern states and Southern disenfranchisement of black voters ran rampant. Southern states began to pass segregation laws that separated blacks from whites on public transportation, restrooms, dining areas, and nearly every other facet of public life. These laws, referred to as **Jim Crow laws,** would remain in place until the Civil Rights Movement. Eighty years later, African Americans would still be fighting for their basic freedoms.

Black soldiers managed to defend their country and their freedom and wage protests against the very government that employed their services.

BLACK SERVICE NEVER FORGOTTEN

In 1913, the United States government organized a gathering of more than fifty thousand Civil War veterans at Gettysburg to mark the fiftieth anniversary of the battle. The event was heartwarming, old gray bearded soldiers embraced; former Confederates and Union veterans enjoyed the festivities. Though the gathering was healing for many, it was incomplete. There were no black veterans present.

Despite the fact that many Americans sought to paint black soldiers as lazy, cowardly, and incompetent, nothing could have been further from the truth. Black soldiers courageously defended not only their country but their right to freedom with less training, less pay, less respect and greater consequences than their white counterparts. Although the United States government and politicians to rewrite history and erase the astonishing achievements of black troops and other minority soldiers who fought, they will be remembered as not only risking more but doing so with less.

Glossary

abolitionist Someone who supports ending slavery.

agency The ability to act in one's own interests.

antebellum The pre-war period, often used in reference to the South prior to the Civil War.

antienticement laws Laws passed by Southern state legislatures that prohibited white people from offering African Americans higher wages or employment opportunities if they were already employed.

apprentice laws Laws passed by southern state legislatures that allowed black children to be taken from their families and put to work if white officials deemed them neglected.

black codes Laws passed across the South to limit the freedoms and movement of black Americans.

Compromise of 1850 This agreement allowed California into the Union in exchange for firmer laws penalizing fugitive slaves and those that assisted their escape.

Compromise of 1877 This informal agreement traded Democrat acceptance of a contested presidential election for the end of Reconstruction.

contraband A term used to refer to runaway slaves who encountered Union troops before they had been freed.

defunct No longer functioning.

Emancipation Proclamation The order given by President Lincoln that declared all slaves in Confederate states free.

Fifteenth Amendment The Constitutional amendment that gave black Americans the right to vote.

First Confiscation Act A Congressional act clarifying the status of fugitive slaves during the Civil War prior to the Emancipation Proclamation.

fortified Strengthened; protected.

Fourteenth Amendment The Constitutional amendment that guaranteed citizenship to those born in the United States.

freedmen A term used to describe freed slaves.

Freedmen's Bureau A post-war government body established for the purpose of easing the transition of freedmen to life as citizens.

Fugitive Slave Law of 1850 A law that required government officials and private citizens to participate in the capture and return of fugitive slaves and stiffened penalties for harboring runaways.

Indian Removal Act Legislation passed by the federal government that allowed for the forcible removal of Native Americans from their homelands.

March to the Sea A military campaign during which William Tecumseh Sherman marched troops through Georgia and South Carolina, leaving destruction in his wake.

parapet A low protective wall meant to safeguard troops.

pig laws Laws passed by Southern state legislatures that applied harsher penalties to theft of livestock or tools, which was often used to falsely imprison African Americans.

prospectors Settlers who moved westward seeking the discovery of gold.

Radical Republicans A group of Republicans that passionately supported and advocated for the rights of freedmen after the Civil War.

Reconstruction The twelve years following the Civil War during which efforts were made to successfully transition from slavery and rebuild the defeated South.

sharecropping A practice in which a farmer does not own the land but works it and gives a percentage to the land's owner as payment for its use.

Special Field Order #15 A military order issued by William Tecumseh Sherman that set aside a large tract of land off the Atlantic coast and army mules for freedmen.

suffrage The right to vote.

Thirteenth Amendment This amendment to the constitution made slavery illegal except in cases where it was used as punishment for a crime.

total war The practice of looting and destroying property in order to demoralize the enemy.

Uncle Tom's Cabin Harriet Beecher Stowe's popular antislavery novel.

vagrancy laws Laws passed by Southern state legislatures that made it illegal for black people to be unemployed.

Bibliography

Baptist, Edward E. *The Half Has Never Been Told: Slavery and the Making of American Capitalism.* New York: Basic, 2016.

Douglass, Frederick, John Stauffer, and Henry Louis Gates. *The Portable Frederick Douglass.* New York: Penguin, 2016.

Escott, Paul David. *Paying Freedom's Price.* New York: Rowman & Littlefield, 2016.

Hansen, Joyce. *Between Two Fires: Black Soliders in the Civil War.* London: Franklin Watts, 1993.

Hine, Darlene Clark., William C. Hine, and Stanley Harrold. *The African-American Odyssey.* Upper Saddle River, NJ: Prentice Hall, 2000.

McPherson, James. "A Brief Overview of the American Civil War." The Civil War Trust. Retrieved November 3, 2016. http://www.civilwar.org/education/history/civil-war-overview/overview.html?referrer=https://www.google.rs/.

National Geographic. "A History of Slavery in the United States." Retrieved November 3, 2016. http://www.nationalgeographic.org/interactive/slavery-united-states/.

National Park Service. "Robert Gould Shaw and the 54th Regiment." Retrieved November 3, 2016. https://www.nps.gov/boaf/learn/historyculture/shaw.htm.

PBS. "The Rise and Fall of Jim Crow." Retrieved November 3, 2016. http://www.pbs.org/wnet/jimcrow/stories_events_freed.html.

Pruitt, Sarah. "Who Was Stand Watie?" The History Channel, June 24, 2015. http://www.history.com/news/who-was-stand-watie.

Smith, John David. *Black Soldiers in Blue: African American Troops in the Civil War Era*. Chapel Hill: University of North Carolina Press, 2002.

Trudeau, Noah Andre. *Like Men of War: Black Troops in the Civil War, 1862–1865*. New York: Back Bay, 1998.

U.S. National Archives and Records Administration. "Black Soldiers in the Civil War." October 3, 2016. https://www.archives.gov/education/lessons/blacks-civil-war.

Warde, Mary Jane. *When the Wolf Came: The Civil War and the Indian Territory*. Fayetteville: University of Arkansas Press, 2013.

 **Further Information**

Books

Berlin, Ira. *The Long Emancipation: The Demise of Slavery in the United States.* Cambridge, MA: Harvard University Press, 2015.

Egerton, Douglas R. *Thunder at The Gates: The Black Civil War Regiments That Redeemed America.* New York: Basic Books, 2016.

Rael, Patrick. *Eighty-Eight Years: The Long Death of Slavery in the United States, 1777–1865.* Athens, GA: University of Georgia Press, 2015.

Sinha, Manisha. *The Slave's Cause: A History of Abolition.* New Haven, CT: Yale University Press, 2016.

Websites

American Civil War

http://www.history.com/topics/american-civil-war

Explore videos, summaries, and photos on this website presented by the History Channel. Topics range from famous battles to Civil War technology.

Civil War Trust

http://www.civilwar.org/

Follow the latest news about Civil War sites and preservation efforts on the Civil War Trust's website.

Slavery by Any Other Name

http://www.pbs.org/tpt/slavery-by-another-name/home/

This PBS website accompanies a documentary of the same title. Navigate timelines, maps, and photo galleries related to slavery and its aftermath.

Videos

"Blood and Glory: The Civil War in Color: Lincoln's Emancipation Proclamation"

https://www.youtube.com/watch?v=XWrQ5VBZi2E

Learn more about the Emancipation Proclamation and the way that Lincoln issued the famous decree.

"Life of the Civil War Soldier – Ranger John Nicholas"

https://www.youtube.com/watch?v=OuAH32LwZ0Q

Gettysburg park ranger John Nicholas provides an in-depth look at the daily lives of Civil War soldiers.

Index

Page numbers in **boldface** are illustrations. Entries in **boldface** are glossary terms.

racism, 22, 33, 37, 50, 96

Radical Republicans, 88

rebellion, 12–13, 37, 48,
  56, 71

Reconstruction, 81, 83,
  87–88, 94, 98

Ross, John, 69, 71, 79

secession, 21, 28–29, 33

sharecropping, 91

Shaw, Robert Gould, 54–55,
  58–59, 62

Sherman, William
  Tecumseh, 47–48, 78,
  90–91

Shiloh, Battle of, 34–35

slave trade, 6–7, 13

Smalls, Robert, 60–61, **61**

Special Field Order #15,
  90–91

St. Catherine's Island, 90–91

Stanton, Edwin, 53

Stowe, Harriet Beecher,
  21–22, 65

suffrage, 20, 92

Thirteenth Amendment,
  92, 94

total war, 47

Trail of Tears, 69

Tubman, Harriet, 17–18, **18**

Turner, Nat, 12–13

Uncle Tom's Cabin, 21, 65

Underground Railroad,
  16–18, 22

United States Navy, 8,
  42–43,

vagrancy laws, 93

Vicksburg, Battle of, 45–46,
  76, 85

wages, 40–42, 55, 86, 93

Watie, Stand, 67, 67, 69–74,
  78–79, 81

westward expansion, 7

Whitney, Eli, 6–7

Wilson's Creek, Battle of, 72

About the Author

Joel Newsome is a writer and history buff living in South Florida. He has written several other books about subjects as diverse as the history of elf mythology and the evolution of the Chumash tribe of Southern California.